Vegan Ketogenic

Smoothies

By: Julian Holden

Please Note

ISBN-13: 978-1544725086
ISBN-10: 1544725086

Contents

Recommendations: 46

1. Chocolate Keto Bomb

Preparation time: 5-10 minutes

Ingredients (makes 1 serving)

- 2 tbsp. chia seeds or
- 2 tbsp coconut butter
- ¼ cup coconut milk
- ¼ cup chocolate hemp protein
- 1 tbsp. extra virgin coconut oil
- 1 tbsp. cacao powder
- 4 drops Stevia extract
- ¼ cup filtered water
- ½ cup ice
- ½ tsp cinnamon or
- A few drops of vanilla extract

Directions

Tip: Make sure to blend well, because coconut oil can solidify as well

Blend smooth and serve immediately!

2. Choco-Berry Cheesecake Smoothie

Preparation time: 5-10 minutes

Ingredients (per serving)

- ¼ cup cashew cheese
- ¼ cup coconut milk
- ½ cup frozen raspberries
- 1 tbsp. cacao powder
- ¾ cup water
- 1 tbsp. Extra virgin coconut oil
- 4 drops liquid Stevia extract

Directions

Place all the ingredients in a blender and Pulse away and enjoy!

3. Chocolate Berry Avocado Smoothie

Ingredients

- ➤ 1 1/3 cup Cashew Milk
- ➤ 1/2 avocado
- ➤ 1/3 cup frozen raspberries & blueberries
- ➤ 1 tbsp cocoa powder
- ➤ 3 drops of stevia
- ➤ 1/8 tsp blueberry extract

Directions

Place all the ingredients in the blender and pulse!

4. Blackberry & Raspberry Vegan Cheesecake Smoothie

Preparation time: 5 minutes

Ingredients (per serving)

- ½ cup blackberries & Raspberry
- ¼ cup full-fat coconut milk
- ¼ cup heavy whipping coconut cream
- ½ cup water
- 1 tbsp MCT oil
- A few drops of Vanilla
- 4 drops liquid Stevia Extract Place all the ingredients in a blender: heavy whipping cream, cream cheese, water, MCT oil, ...

Directions

Add ingredients to blender and pulse.

5. Spring Redcurrant Smoothie

Preparation time: 5 minutes

Ingredients (per serving)

- ½ cup redcurrants, fresh or frozen
- 2 large Fresh strawberries
- ¼ cup coconut milk
- ½ cup water
- 3 tbsp. chia seeds
- ½ vanilla bean
- 4 drops liquid Stevia extract

Directions

Place all the ingredients into a blender and pulse until smooth Also please allow to set and settle a little bit!

6.   Fresh Keto Berry Shake

Preparation time: 5-10 minutes

Ingredients

- ¼ cup creamed coconut milk
- ½ cup almond milk
- ½ cup fresh mixed berries
- 1 tbsp. MCT oil
- ½ cup ice
- 4 drops Stevia extract
- ½ tsp vanilla extract
- Whipped Coconut Cream on top

Directions

To cream the coconut milk just allow coconut milk can in the refrigerator overnight the spoon it hard solid piece of coconut milk and throw away liquids. Make sure not shake before opening.

Add ingredients into a blender and pulse.

Pulse until smooth and serve immediately. Optionally, top with whipped cream or coconut milk.

7. Coconut Vegan Strawberry Smoothie

Preparation time: 5-10 minutes

Ingredients

- ¾ cup strawberries Fresh or Frozen
- 1 cup of coconut milk
- 2 tablespoons smooth cashew butter
- 2 packets stevia or 3-4 drops stevia drops

Directions

Add all ingredients to blender.

Then Blend!

And Enjoy!

8. Low-Carb Strawberry & Rhubarb Pie Smoothie

Preparation time: 5 minutes

Ingredients

- 2 medium strawberries
- 1 medium rhubarb stalks
- 2 tbsp. almond butter
- 2 tbsp. of chia seeds
- ½ cup almond milk
- 3 tbsp. coconut milk
- 1 tsp thinly grated fresh ginger root
- ½ tsp pure vanilla bean extract
- 5 drops liquid Stevia extract

Directions

Add all the ingredients into a blender and pulse!

Enjoy!

9.   Berry Avocado Smoothie

Ingredients

- ➤ 1/2 ripe avocado peeled and pit removed
- ➤ 1 cup water
- ➤ 3 tablespoons lemon juice
- ➤ 3-4 drops of stevia
- ➤ 1/2 cup frozen Mixed Berries

Directions

Place all ingredients to blender.

Blend until smooth.

Enjoy!

10. Keto Frozen Mint Hot Chocolate

Ingredients

➢ 1 cup unsweetened almond milk
➢ 3-4 ounces dark chocolate 90%, chopped
➢ 1/2 cup Brown Rice Protein powder
➢ 1/2 tsp peppermint extract
➢ 1 tsp liquid stevia
➢ 1½ cups ice

Directions

Add all ingredients in blender and pulse.

Optional: Top With Whipped Coconut Cream!

11. Chocolate Macadamia Smoothie

Preparation time: 5-10 min

Ingredients

- ➢ 1 1/3 cup ice cubes
- ➢ 2/3 cup coconut milk
- ➢ 3 tbsp. crushed macadamia nuts
- ➢ 3-4 Stevia drops
- ➢ 1 tbsp. unsweetened cocoa powder
- ➢ 1/2 tsp vanilla extract

Directions

Blend the ingredients into smooth.

Optional: Top with whipped coconut cream, and add crushed macadamia nuts.

12. Chocolate Almond Butter Milkshake

Preparation time: 5 min

Ingredients

- ¾ cup coconut milk
- ¾ tablespoon unsweetened cocoa powder
- 2 tablespoons Almond Butter
- 4 drops Stevia Drops
- Dash Pink Salt

Directions

Place all ingredients in blender and pulse.

Enjoy!

13. Keto Cherry Chocolate Post Workout Smoothie

Ingredients

- 1/2 cup fresh pitted cherries
- ¾ cup coconut milk
- 1 scoop soy protein
- ½ cup hemp hearts
- 1/5 cup unsweetened cocoa powder
- 4 drops stevia drops
- 1 cup ice
- 2-4 pieces of 85% dark chocolate

Directions

Place all ingredients in blender and pulse!

Enjoy!

14. Chocolate Green Smoothie

Preparation time: 5-10 minutes

Ingredients

- 1/2 cup of sliced apples of choice
- 3/4 cup coconut cream
- 100g spinach chopped
- 1/4 cup cocoa powder
- 3-4 Squares of 85% dark chocolate
- 2-3 drops of stevia sweetener

Directions

Put everything in a blender and blend till smooth!

Enjoy!

15. Latin Chocolate Shake

Preparation time: 5-10 minutes

Ingredients (per serving)

- ¼ cup coconut cream
- 1 ½ tbsp. extra virgin coconut oil
- 1 tbsp. ground chia seeds soaked for 5 min before
- 2 ½ tbsp. Cacao powder
- ¼ tsp organic vanilla extract
- ¼ tsp cinnamon powder
- ¼ tsp cayenne powder
- 1 cup of water
- ½ cup ice

Directions

Put all the ingredients in a blender, pulse until smooth.

16. LOW CARB GREEN SMOOTHIE

Preparation time: 5 mins

Ingredients (makes 1 serving)

- ➤ 2 cups spinach
- ➤ 1½ cups ice
- ➤ 1 cup almond milk
- ➤ ½ avocado, pitted and scooped out
- ➤ ¼ cup brown rice protein powder
- ➤ 4 stevia drops

Directions

Add ingredients in blender and Pulse!

Enjoy!

17. Irish Pre-Workout Keto Bomb

Ingredients

- 1/2 cup avocado
- ½ tbs. MCT oil
- 1/2 cup unsweetened almond milk
- ½ cup black coffee
- 1 scoop soy protein
- 1 TBS cashew cheese
- 1 cup crushed ice
- 4 drops stevia
- 1 tablespoon fresh mint leaves
- 1/2 tsp Celtic Sea Salt

Directions

Place ingredients into blender and Pulse!

Enjoy!

18. Vanilla Green Smoothie

Ingredients

- ➢ 1 cup unsweetened vanilla almond milk
- ➢ 2 ice cubes
- ➢ 2 1/2 cups of spinach
- ➢ 1/2 of an avocado
- ➢ 1 tbsp. of ground flax seeds
- ➢ 4 drops of vanilla stevia

Directions

Place ingredients into blender and Pulse!

Enjoy!

19. Green Keto Atomic Bomb

Ingredients

- 1 cup water
- 1 cup romaine lettuce
- 1 cup kale chopped
- 1 cup spinach
- ⅓ cup chopped fresh pineapple
- 2 Tbsp fresh parsley
- ¾ Tbsp. fresh ginger, peeled and chopped
- 1 cup raw cucumber, peeled and sliced
- ½ cup kiwi fruit, peeled and chopped
- ½ small avocado
- 4 drops of stevia

Directions

Place ingredients into blender and Pulse!

Enjoy!

20. Leprechaun Keto Smoothie

Preparation time: 5 minutes

Ingredients (per serving)

➤ ½ avocado
➤ ¼ cup coconut milk
➤ ½ cup fresh baby spinach
➤ 2 Leaves of fresh mint
➤ 1 scoop of hemp protein
➤ 3 tbsp. pistachio nuts
➤ 1 vanilla bean
➤ 4 drops liquid Stevia extract
➤ ½ water
➤ ½ cup of ice

Directions

Place ingredients into blender and Pulse!

Enjoy!

21. Matcha Keto Smoothie

Preparation time: 5-10 minutes

Ingredients (makes 1 serving)

- ½ avocado
- ¾ cup fresh spinach
- ½ cup coconut milk
- ¾ cup of water
- ½ cup of ice
- 1 tsp vanilla extract
- 1 tbsp. extra virgin coconut oil
- 4 drops of stevia extract
- 1 tsp matcha green tea powder

Directions

Place ingredients into blender and Pulse!

Enjoy!

22. Keto Aussie Smoothie

Preparation time: 5 minutes

Ingredients (per serving)

- ¼ avocado
- ¼ cup coconut milk
- 1 small Slice of Honeydew
- ¼ cup kiwi fruit
- 1 scoop of hemp protein
- 1 tbsp. soaked chia seeds (for thickness)
- 4 drops liquid Stevia
- ½ cup water
- ½ cup of ice

Directions

Place ingredients into blender and Pulse!

Enjoy!

23. Green Tea Energy Shake

Yield: 2 smoothies

A low carb avocado green tea smoothie, packed with protein and anti-oxidants. The ultimate post-workout recovery drink! Sugar-free.

Ingredients

- 1 tsp matcha green tea powder
- 1 tbsp. warm water
- 1/2 avocado
- 1/2 cup Coconut yogurt
- 1 scoop of soy protein
- 4 Stevia extract drops
- 1 cup almond milk

Directions

In a bowl, whisk together matcha powder and warm water. Let it sit for 5 minutes then add to blender.

Add all the ingredients together and pulse.

Enjoy!

24. Acai Keto Smoothie Bowl

Preparation time: 5-10 minutes

Ingredients

Smoothie Bowl Base

- ¾ cup spinach
- 1/2 cup almond milk
- 2 tbsp. coconut cream
- 1/2 tbsp. coconut oil
- 1 scoop brown rice protein
- 3 ice cubes
- Small Package Acai

Toppings

- 6 walnuts
- 2 tbsp. shredded coconut
- 1 tsp chia seeds

Directions

Add spinach into blender with coconut milk, cream, oil and ice. Blend into a frothy creamy consistency.

Pour the mixture in a medium bowl.

Lightly blend acai.

Add walnuts, shredded coconut and chia seeds.

Enjoy your quick, easy and healthy smoothie bowl!

25. Almond Butter Banana Chia Smoothie

Ingredients

- ➢ 3/4 cup Coconut yogurt
- ➢ 3/4 cup almond milk
- ➢ 3 tbsp. Almond butter
- ➢ 3 tbsp. chia seeds
- ➢ 1/3 tsp banana extract
- ➢ 4 drops liquid stevia extract

Directions

In a bowl, whisk together matcha powder and warm water. Let it sit for 5 minutes then add to blender.

Add all the ingredients together and pulse.

Enjoy!

26. Keto Vegan Hangover Smoothie

Ingredients

- 2 Slices of Soy Bacon
- 1/2 Cup Almond Milk
- 1/4 Cup Frozen blueberries
- 1/2 Cup Coconut yogurt
- 1/2 Avocado
- 1/3 Teaspoon of Cinnamon
- 1/4 Teaspoon of Salt
- 4 drops of Stevia Extract

Directions

To Create

Cook bacon and put aside.

Blend cocktail Ingredients (except for soy bacon)

Next Step

Add all the ingredients together in blender expect bacon and pulse.

Eat bacon when done. Enjoy!

27. Classic Peanut Butter Smoothie

Ingredients

- 1/2 cup unsweetened almond milk
- 1 tablespoon natural peanut butter, no sugar added
- ½ cup ice
- ½ cup water
- 4 droppers Stevia extract
- 1 scoop of brown rice protein

Directions

Add all the ingredients together in blender and pulse.

Enjoy!

28. Keto Vanilla Bean Frappuccino

Ingredients

- 3/4 cup unsweetened vanilla almond milk
- 1/3 cup of coconut milk
- 1 vanilla bean scraped out
- ½ teaspoon vanilla liquid stevia
- ½ cup of ice
- Coconut Cream

Directions

Add all ingredients expect ice.

Pulse on high.

Add ice and pulse again for 20-30 seconds to crush ice.

Adding whipped Coconut Cream on top.

29. Vanilla Keto Smoothie

Preparation time: 5-10 minutes

Ingredients

- ➤ 2 tbsp. chia seeds soaked for 1 minute
- ➤ ½ cup coconut milk
- ➤ 1 scoop of vanilla soy protein
- ➤ 1 tbsp. MCT oil
- ➤ 1 tsp vanilla extract
- ➤ 4 drops Stevia extract
- ➤ ½ cup water
- ➤ ½ cup ice

Directions

Place ingredients into blender and Pulse!

Enjoy!

30. Pumpkin Keto Smoothie

Ingredients

- ½ cup unsweetened vanilla almond milk
- ¾ cup canned pumpkin
- 2 oz. cashew cheese
- 1 scoop of vanilla soy protein
- ½ cup of water
- 1/2 cup crushed ice
- 4 drops of stevia extract

Directions

Place ingredients into blender and Pulse!

Enjoy!

31. Cinnamon Roll Ketone Rush

Ingredients

➢ 1 cup almond milk
➢ 1 tbsp. MCT
➢ 1 tbsp. Brain Octane Oil
➢ ½ tsp. cinnamon
➢ ¼ tsp. vanilla extract
➢ 4 teaspoons sweetener
➢ 1 tsp. flax meal
➢ 1 tsp. chia seeds
➢ ½ cup of ice
➢ ½ cup of water

Directions

Place ingredients into blender and Pulse!

Enjoy!

32. Keto Butternut Squash Smoothie

Preparation time: 5-10 minutes

Ingredients

- ¼ cup boiled & chilled butternut squash
- ¼ cup unsweetened almond milk
- 1 scoop brown rice protein
- ¼ cup coconut milk
- ½ tsp pumpkin pie spice mix
- 4 drops liquid stevia
- 1 tbsp. Extra virgin coconut oil
- ¼ cup whipped coconut nut cream

Directions

Place ingredients into blender and Pulse!

Enjoy!

33. Keto Cinco De Mayo Smoothie

Preparation time: 10-15 minutes

Ingredients (makes 2 servings)

- ➢ 2 handfuls almonds
- ➢ 1 cup almond milk unsweetened
- ➢ 2 tbsp. ground chia seeds
- ➢ 1 tbsp. lime zest freshly grated
- ➢ ½ tsp cinnamon
- ➢ 2 cups warm water (480 ml / 16.2 fl oz)

Directions

Place ingredients into blender and Pulse!

Enjoy!

34. Keto Vegan Lasi

Ingredients

- ➢ 2 cups ice cold water
- ➢ 200 grams of Coconut yogurt
- ➢ 1/4 teaspoon pink salt
- ➢ 3-4 drops stevia extract

Directions

Place ingredients into blender and Pulse!

Enjoy!

35. Rose Water Sweet Lasi

Ingredients

- 2 cups cold water
- 200 grams of coconut yogurt
- 1 organic green cardamom pod
- 1 teaspoon organic rose water
- 3-4 extracts of stevia extract

Directions

Place ingredients into blender and Pulse!

Enjoy!

36. Mint Lassi

Ingredients

- ➤ 2 cups cold water
- ➤ 200 grams of coconut yogurt
- ➤ 2-4 fresh, organic mint leaves
- ➤ 4 drops of stevia extract

Directions

Place all ingredients in blender and pulse!

Enjoy!

37. Nut Orange Lassi

Ingredients

- ➢ 2 cups cold water
- ➢ 200 grams of coconut yogurt
- ➢ 1/3 teaspoon almond extract
- ➢ 1/3 teaspoon orange blossom water
- ➢ 4 Stevia extract drops

Directions

Add all in ingredients into blender and pulse!

Enjoy!

38. Berry Cantaloupe Lassi

Ingredients

- ➤ 2 cups of cold water
- ➤ ½ cup blueberries
- ➤ 200 grams of coconut yogurt
- ➤ ½ cup cantaloupe chunks
- ➤ 4 stevia extract drops

Directions

Add all ingredients into blender and pulse!

Enjoy!

39. Orange Lassi

Ingredients

- ➢ 2 cups cold water
- ➢ 200 grams coconut yogurt
- ➢ Freshly grated orange
- ➢ 1 tbsp. freshly grated ginger
- ➢ 4 drops of stevia

Directions

Place all ingredients in blender and pulse!

Enjoy!

40. Coconut Milk Kefir

Preparation time: 24 hours

Ingredients (makes 4 cups)

- ➢ 4 cups coconut milk
- ➢ 1 sachet kefir starter cultures

Directions

Cover it leaving a little room to breathe and leave at room temperature for 24 hours in in the oven with light turned on. The best temperature for making kefir is around 22 C.

When done, shake and add to refrigerator.

Enjoy!

Recommendations:

Please click on the link below to be taken to my recommendations page to have the best tools to create your perfect low carb vegan recipes as well some great further reading recommendations:

http://bit.ly/veganketo1

48858209R00028

Made in the USA
Middletown, DE
29 September 2017